For Constance, Carolyn, Cynthia,

Michael, Daniel, and Colin

more small poems

by Valerie Worth
pictures by Natalie Babbitt

Farrar, Straus and Giroux   New York

Poems copyright © 1976 by Valerie Worth
Pictures copyright © 1976 by Natalie Babbitt
All rights reserved
Published simultaneously in Canada by
McGraw-Hill Ryerson Ltd., Toronto
Printed in the United States of America
First edition, 1976
Library of Congress Cataloging
in Publication Data
Worth, Valerie / More Small Poems
[1. American Poetry]
I. Babbitt, Natalie / II. Title
PZ8.3.W913Mo / [811] / 76-28323

more small poems

magnifying glass 1

kitten 2

safety pin 4

earthworms 5

lawnmower 7

sparrow 8

magnet 10

lions 13

acorn 14

caterpillar 16

fireworks 19

flamingo 20

hose 22

mosquito 24

shoes 25

sea lions 27

sidewalks 28

crab 30

weeds 31

haunted house 33

toad 34

pumpkin 35

christmas lights 37

dinosaurs 39

soap bubble 41

magnifying glass

Small grains
In a stone
Grow edges
That twinkle;

The smooth
Moth's wing
Sprouts feathers
Like shingles;

My thumb
Is wrapped
In rich
Satin wrinkles.

kitten

The black kitten,
Arched stiff,
Dances sidewise
From behind
The chair, leaps,
Tears away with
Ears back, spins,
Lands crouched
Flat on the floor,
Sighting something
At nose level,

Her eyes round
As oranges, her
Hind legs marking
Time: then she
Pounces, cactus-
Clawed, upon
A strayed
Strand of fluff:
Can anyone
Believe that she
Doesn't ask us
To laugh?

safety pin

Closed, it sleeps
On its side
Quietly,
The silver
Image
Of some
Small fish;

Opened, it snaps
Its tail out
Like a thin
Shrimp, and looks
At the sharp
Point with a
Surprised eye.

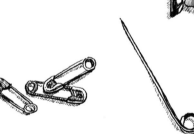

earthworms

Garden soil,
Spaded up,
Gleams with
Gravel-glints,
Mica-sparks, and
Bright wet
Glimpses of
Earthworms
Stirring beneath:

Put on the palm,
Still rough
With crumbs,
They roll and
Glisten in the sun
As fresh
As new rubies
Dug out of
Deepest earth.

lawnmower

The lawnmower
Grinds its teeth
Over the grass,
Spitting out a thick
Green spray;

Its head is too full
Of iron and oil
To know
What it throws
Away:

The lawn's whole
Crop of chopped,
Soft,
Delicious
Green hay.

sparrow

Nothing is less
Rare than
One dust-
Colored sparrow
In a driveway
Minding her own
Matters, pottering
Carelessly, finding
Seeds in the tire-
Flattened weeds:

But because
She can dare
To let us watch her
There, when all
The stately robins
Have fled
Scolding into
The air, she
Is as good a bird
As anyone needs.

magnet

This small
Flat horseshoe
Is sold for
A toy: we are
Told that it
Will pick up pins
And it does, time
After time; later
It lies about,
Getting its red
Paint chipped, being
Offered pins less
Often, until at
Last we leave it
Alone: then

It leads its own
Life, trading
Secrets with
The North Pole,
Reading
Invisible messages
From the sun.

lions

Bars, wire,
Glass, and rails, and
Even two men
Washing down
The concrete cells
Toward gutter tiles
Where the water
Flows away,

Cannot keep
From the aisles
The harsh gold
Smell of lions,
Luckily: otherwise
They could be heavy
Puppets of plush-
Covered clay.

acorn

An acorn
Fits perfectly
Into its shingled
Cup, with a stick
Attached
At the top,

Its polished
Nut curves
In the shape
Of a drop, drawn
Down to a thorn
At the tip,

And its heart
Holds folded
Thick white fat
From which
A marvelous
Tree grows up:

I think no better
Invention or
Mechanical trick
Could ever
Be bought
In a shop.

caterpillar

The feet of the
Caterpillar
Do not patter
As he passes
Like the clever
Quick paws
Of the squirrel,
But they ripple,
Stepping one pair
After another
And another,
And they travel
With his whole
Long caravan
Of bristles
Down the brown
Twig, to a
Greener midsummer
Dinner.

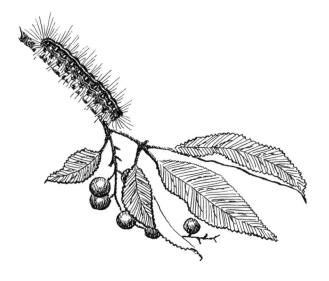

fireworks

First
A far thud,
Then the rocket
Climbs the air,
A dull red flare,
To hang, a moment,
Invisible, before
Its shut black shell cracks
And claps against the ears,
Breaks and billows into bloom,
Spilling down clear green sparks, gold spears,
Silent sliding silver waterfalls and stars.

flamingo

The
Flamingo
Lingers
A
Long
Time
Over
One
Pink
Leg;

Later
He
Ponders
Upon
The
Other
For
A
While
Instead.

hose

The hose
Can squeeze
Water to
A silver rod
That digs
Hard holes
In the mud,

Or, muzzled
Tighter by
The nozzle,
Can rain
Chill diamond
Chains
Across the yard,

Or, fanned
Out fine,
Can hang
A silk
Rainbow
Halo
Over soft fog.

mosquito

There is more
To a mosquito
Than her sting
Or the way she sings
In the ear:

There are her wings
As clear
As windows,
There are the sleek
Velvets on her back;

She bends six
Slender knees,
And her eye, that
Sees the swatter,
Glitters.

shoes

Which to prefer?
Hard leather heels,
Their blocks carved
Thick, like rocks,
Clacked down
Waxed wood stairs,

Or the pale soles
Of sneakers,
Worn smooth, soft
As mushroom caps,
Supple upon warm
Summer pavements?

sea lions

The satin sea lions
Nudge each other
Toward the edge
Of the pool until
They fall like
Soft boulders
Into the water,
Sink down, slide
In swift circles,
Twist together
And apart, rise again
Snorting, climb
Up slapping
Their flippers on
The wet cement:
Someone said
That in all the zoo
Only the sea lions
Seem happy.

sidewalks

Sidewalks wear out;
Some sunk squares,
Winter-cracked,
Even break:
Then their chunks
Tip up
To trip old women,
Scrape the bare
Big toe, stop
Skates that rolled
Rits, rits, before,
And slow them
To step
Dit dit dit around.

crab

The dead crab
Lies still,
Limp on dry sand,

All strength to crawl
Gone from his
Hard shell—

But he keeps a shape
Of old anger
Curved along his claws.

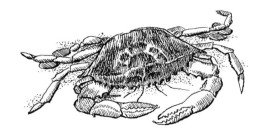

weeds

In the rough places,
Along concrete curbs,
Up railroad banks,
Next to brick buildings,
Weeds will grow;
And no one cares
If they live there,
Year after year:
Quietly attending
To roots, stalks,
Or even, above
Dusty leaves, a few
Dim stars of flowers.

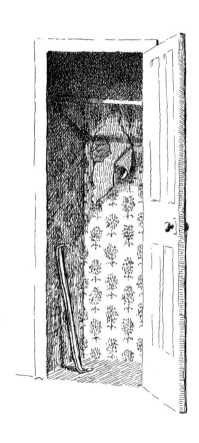

haunted house

Its echoes,
Its aching stairs,
Its doors gone stiff
At the hinges,

Remind us of its
Owners, who
Grew old, who
Died, but

Who are still
Here: leaning
In the closet like
That curtain rod,

Sleeping on the cellar
Shelf like this
Empty
Jelly jar.

toad

When the flowers
Turned clever, and
Earned wide
Tender red petals
For themselves,

When the birds
Learned about feathers,
Spread green tails,
Grew cockades
On their heads,

The toad said:
Someone has got
To remember
The mud, and
I'm not proud.

pumpkin

After its lid
Is cut, the slick
Seeds and stuck
Wet strings
Scooped out,
Walls scraped
Dry and white,
Face carved, candle
Fixed and lit,

Light creeps
Into the thick
Rind: giving
That dead orange
Vegetable skull
Warm skin, making
A live head
To hold its
Sharp gold grin.

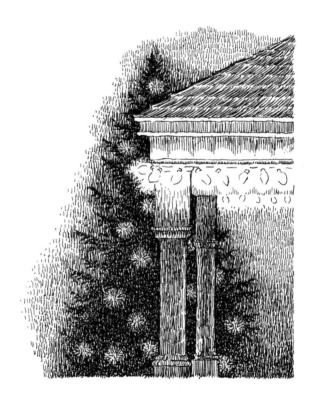

christmas lights

Bulbs strung along
Our porch roof
Pour clear
Colors through the
Cold black air;

But our neighbors
Have a spruce, like
A huge shadow,
Full of deep blue
Mysterious stars.

dinosaurs

Dinosaurs
Do not count,
Because
They are all
Dead:

None of us
Saw them, dogs
Do not even
Know that
They were there—

But they
Still walk
About heavily
In everybody's
Head.

soap bubble

The soap bubble's
Great soft sphere
Bends out of shape
On the air,
Leans, rounds again,
Rises, shivering, heavy,
A planet revolving
Hollow and clear,
Mapped with
Rainbows, streaming,
Curled: seeming
A world too splendid
To snap, dribble,
And disappear.